The Loki Variations

Published by 404 Ink Limited
www.404Ink.com
@404Ink

Editing & proofreading: Heather McDaid
Typesetting: Laura Jones
Cover design: Luke Bird
Co-founders and publishers of 404 Ink:
Heather McDaid & Laura Jones

Print ISBN: 978-1-912489-68-8
Ebook ISBN: 978-1-912489-69-5

Printed and bound in Great Britain by Clays Ltd, Elcograf S.p.A.

The Loki Variations

The Man, The Myth, The Mischief

Karl Johnson

Inklings

For my peerie Freyr

Contents

Spoiler Notes

As well as exploring Norse mythology, details for Loki-related pop culture are highlighted to various degrees (some important, some not) throughout *The Loki Variations*. Most mentions are brief, but be aware…

Chapter 1:
Loki Season 1 (TV show, 2021)
Loki: A Bad God's Guide to Being Good (book, 2022)
Ragnarok: The End of The Gods (book, 2011)
The Gospel of Loki (book, 2014)
The Trials of Loki (comic, 2011)

Chapter 2:
Avengers #1 (comic, 1963)
Avengers Assemble (movie, 2012)
Journey Into Mystery #111 (comic, 1962)
Loki Season 1 (TV show, 2021)
Loki: Agent of Asgard – The Complete Collection (comic, 2020)
Loki: Journey Into Mystery Omnibus (comic, 2017)
Loki: Mistress of Mischief (comic, 2021) collecting select issues of *Thor* (2007-2009)

Loki: Where Mischief Lies (novel, 2019)
Marvel Loki Omnibus Vol. 1 (comic, 2021)
Original Sin #5.5 (comic, 2014)
Thor (movie, 2011)
Thor: The Dark World (movie, 2013)
Thor: Ragnarok (movie, 2017)

Chapter 3:

Loki Season 1 (TV show, 2021)
Loki: The God Who Fell to Earth #5 (comic, 2019)
Ragnarok (TV show, 2020-2022)
Supernatural (TV show, 2005-2020)
The Gospel of Loki (book, 2014)
The Mythical Detective Loki Ragnarok (Manga, 1999-2004)

Chapter 4:

American Gods (book, 2001)
Eight Days of Luke (book, 1975)
Loki: A Bad God's Guide to Being Good (book, 2022)
Loki: A Bad God's Guide to Taking the Blame (book, 2022)
Loki: Agent of Asgard – The Complete Collection (comic, 2020)
Odd and the Frost Giants (book, 2008)
Orkanpartyt, or, The Hurricane Party (book, 2007)
Ragnarok: The End of The Gods (book, 2011)
The Gospel of Loki (book, 2014)

(Dis)Honourable Mentions

Dogma (movie, 1999)
Jay and Silent Bob Reboot (movie, 2019)
Jul I Valhal, or, Christmas in Valhalla (TV show, 2005)
Son of The Mask (movie, 2005)
Thor: Love and Thunder (movie, 2022)
Thor: Ragnarok (movie, 2017)

NB: I've tried to be consistent in using they/them pronouns when referring to the core, OG, mythological Loki from the Eddas, but otherwise by following how the variations present themselves.

Introduction

I've come to terms with the fact that I'll never see a Marvel movie where Tom Hiddleston transforms into a mare to procreate with the horse of a giant stonemason, before giving birth to an eight-legged steed and gifting it to his father. The Marvel Cinematic Universe (MCU) version of Loki is just not the Norse god I grew up with. Neither is Luke, the isolated fire-starter from Diana Wynne Jones's children's novel *Eight Days of Luke*, nor the expositional plot-device personified by The Trickster/Archangel Gabriel from long-running TV series *Supernatural*, and certainly not the bratty sidekick Atreus in the *God of War* videogames. Contemporary popular culture is awash with countless adaptations, interpretations, re-imaginings, versions – variations, if you will – of the character of Loki from Norse mythology.

These variations on the Loki from legend (which is itself open to interpretation) tend to focus, variously, on some key aspects that are assumed to be core to who the god is; mischief, lies, evil, shapeshifting, gender fluidity, magic, hidden agendas, emotional outbursts, rebellion, humour, and psychopathy. In our shared consciousness Loki is simultaneously a hero, anti-hero, villain, and neutral observer. Norse gods Odin and Thor are usually connected in some way, too, although the sibling- and/or parent-child dynamics change depending on which Loki we are presented with. As is often the case with characters in the public domain (like Sherlock Holmes) and some who have been through several iterations over generations (like Doctor Who), every Loki variation is Someone's Loki – every Loki variation is thus equally valid. Every Loki variation has a purpose, a function, a reason why they have been presented the way they have and a motive behind the story they're a part of. Obviously, the main motives are to appeal to particular audiences and make money, but beyond that there are opportunities to talk about the environment (as in the Netflix series *Ragnarok*), gender and sexuality (as is increasingly, tentatively seen in Marvel's comics, TV and movie output), and the power of faith (or lack thereof, as in Neil Gaiman's *American Gods*).

Loki is often an unreliable narrator, but these variations can help us uncover many truths about our society, history, and culture. They can function as a tool to help explore the power of myth, queer theory, fandom, ritual, popular culture itself, and more.

I'm still conflicted, though. The Loki I grew up with was folklore, while the one that lives in my head now is a license for Disney to print money. I discovered my Loki in the mythology books in my school library; a mercurial godling who played the fool but didn't suffer them. While not the most powerful Norse god, the Loki I was introduced to certainly wielded more influence and intelligence than most and rebelled against the constraints of convention. My Loki was felt in the background of the Viking-inspired Up Helly Aa fire festival in the Shetland parish I grew up in, with the ceremonial shield depicting Loki's horse-child Sleipnir. Over the years though, I've lost a clear sense of my Loki from the library and their voice – it's been gradually replaced by the omnipresence of the Marvel variations of Loki. I feel I need that time back, to rediscover the core of the cunning red-haired trickster I first met. Luckily, we have the time here, and as Loki says in Snorri Sturluson's *The Poetic Edda,* 'I intend to live for a good time yet…'[1]

How to unpack the Loki variations, then? We need to go back to the beginning, or, more accurately, a version of the retelling of the beginning, with what we know about Loki from Norse mythology. From the core *Eddas* Loki of the 13th century, who provides the earliest and most fully-formed variation we can reliably interrogate, we'll move onto those that have appeared in pop culture in living memory, seeking out commonalities as well as distinct outliers. I'm interested in exploring what Loki, in any and all variations, can tell us from sociocultural perspectives – how can Loki help to contextualise and evidence how we understand contemporary society and our lived reality? How does Loki, specifically, and mythology and pop culture more broadly, connect how we understand ourselves with how we engage with others? Selfishly, my secondary hope is that in researching and writing this I can better understand the nature of the Norse influence in my own identity and reconcile how ingrained or invented the significance of Loki is to that.

I'm from Shetland, a group of islands in the North Sea, sitting to the far north of Scotland and west of Norway. Norse – or perhaps more accurately, Viking – imagery is everywhere in Shetland, in our schools and museums, our music and literature, and in our local businesses and tourism. Although UK citizens, Shetlanders can make genuine claims to ancient Nordic heritage, evidenced in the Old Norse retained in Shetland dialect and place-names,[2] local traditions and folklore,[3] and art and design.[4]

Like other Shetland children, I have grown up thinking that it was normal for homes to have decorative shields and axes on the wall. The way we internalise our distant Norse heritage is built around a caricature, in many respects, and so any deeper understanding and emotional investment relies on individual interest and study in the mythology, culture and history of the time. I do wonder whether we should be making more of a concerted effort to do this, as all too often the complex messages and questions behind Norse mythology are ignored in favour of simplified notions of heroes, villains, and monsters.

Popular culture is not just all the geeky stuff that many of us enjoy. In truth it encompasses a seemingly endless array of cultural objects, texts, practices, and beliefs; its forms are those that are dominant, common or far-reaching in everyday society and so are recognised and shared among us. By understanding pop culture as a contemporary folklore that we imbue with personal and shared meaning, we lay the groundwork for why Loki is particularly skilled in shape-shifting and resurrecting themselves across different genres and platforms. Pop culture is distinctly not high culture (which we might think of as forms that are exclusive and elitist, appreciated for their aesthetic and/or intellectual value), nor is it strictly class-based although it's not typically associated with upper class cultural tastes. Pop culture takes many forms; television, cinema, music, fiction, comics, games, sports, news, fashion, technology, and in the activities and communication built around them – including slang and memes.[5] Mass produced and commodified in most cases, many social and cultural thinkers of the 20th century – such as Theodor Adorno and Max Horkheimer – were dismissive of popular/mass culture as a by-product of the commercialisation and lack of authenticity increasingly found in the consumerism enabled by the Western industrial revolution.[6]

What they missed (and others thankfully recognised), however, was that the production of pop culture doesn't solely create profit – it creates connections between people in everyday life and cements relationships, establishes universal forms of language and shared purposes, and helps explain and maintain our identities. To truly understand the history and politics of society, one must understand popular culture. The ubiquity of pop culture means that it is in the escapism of a comic, or the characters in a TV show, or the lyrics of a song, that we encode the everyday human experience. Questions of power, ideology, family, and so much more, can be explored in the accessible cultural canons that we love, with impact and reach that the Tate galleries can only dream of.[7] Cultural theorist Stuart Hall wrote about how the encoding and decoding of pop culture materials is a process of meaningful communication, via forms such as TV news coverage, by which we create shared knowledge and perspectives as a kind of social project. Hall cites an example from essayist Roland Barthes, of the symbolism associated with a sweater. The sweater, as a mass-produced object, is simply a warm garment but also indicates the action of staying warm, and so further suggests cold weather or even the Winter season.[8]

Barthes' approach is important in helping us unpack the Loki variations. In his book *Mythologies*, Barthes looks at how contemporary Western society has created its own modern myths in a series of essays on forms of popular culture ranging from wrestling to astrology, via washing powder and striptease.[9] The more traditional purpose of mythology has been in guiding cultural interpretations of right/wrong and good/evil, offering cautionary tales and explaining everyday phenomena in ways that avoid complication. Over time the historical contexts in which myths have formed, and the representative ways that they have established, have increasingly taken on ideological powers in everyday discourse and found themselves reshaped to fit contemporary social and political narratives. Myths, historical or contemporary, are often a means by which a more conservative status quo can maintain dominance in our collective consciousness, and so it is in the telling and retelling of myths that our lived social reality is founded on values rather than facts.[10]

Here we find ourselves at the end of the beginning, appropriately enough, with more questions than answers. There is power in myth, that much is clear. Contemporary societies can consume and (re)create myth via a multitude of pop culture forms, and in many respects it would appear that we do this out of necessity as much as we do it for pleasure.

Who is Loki? There is no single true form of a myth; instead there can be many different variations, so long as each variation feels like it could recognisably be The Myth. As long as the constituent parts are broadly similar and/or the function of each variation has a shared sense of purpose, then every(one's) Loki can be a legitimate Loki.

Who is your Loki? There are a number of well-known variations: Gods of Knots, Fire, Mischief, Outcasts, and Stories; Princes of Evil, and Lies; Lords and Ladies; heroes and villains; children (people have started naming their babies Loki at a modest but reliable rate[11][12]); cats, dogs, and alligators. They surely have different roles to fulfil, just as much as lesser-known variations do, like the Loki who is a paranormal detective trapped in the body of a child, from Japanese manga and anime.

And who is my Loki, and what is their glorious purpose? Let's journey into mystery, together, and find out.

Chapter 1
God of Knots

Loki is known in many forms and by several names; simultaneously chaotic, calculating, villainous, heroic, outgoing and mysterious. These contradictions and complexities exist in a mass to be untangled. With no singular thread, or unifying story, these knots see Loki as a malleable character who is bent into many forms. They are known to many as the God of Mischief, but that was not always so. This is part of the tricky problem of Loki folklore; nothing is necessarily straightforward or definitive and I already regret trying to tackle this at all. But this is also part of what makes it fascinating to me. So, before we go any further, let's bear the following in mind.

Norse mythology wasn't concerned with its deities as being The God of (insert descriptor here) in quite the same way as one might think of the Greek or Roman legends. Thor, for example, was not (at least it would seem) explicitly The God of Thunder, but rather God of the Sky, bringing fine seasons and fair winds to farmers and sailors respectively. Thor was a charioteer and a champion of Asgard, renowned for battling giants and over-indulging himself. Similarly, Loki was never the God of Mischief, although they made plenty of it.

The word 'mischief' is doing a considerable amount of work, seeking to account for things like practical jokes that went too far, putting the Norse gods (individually and collectively) at risk of harm and/or death, verbally roasting friends in one particularly vicious example, and simply being queer.

These statements, and much else, are based almost entirely on the retellings of one person, who was perhaps not entirely reliable himself, Snorri Sturluson.

Snorri is generally accredited with composing *The Prose* and *The Poetic Eddas* – manuscripts written in 13th century Iceland, recording collections of stories and poems from which our knowledge of Norse mythology is derived – although it can't be said with absolute certainty whether he actually wrote them or rather curated pre-existing literature. It's reasonable to assume that the *Eddas* are fairly representative of the oral tradition of Scandinavian peoples of what we might call the Viking Age, approximately from 800 to

1100 AD. For many, the *Eddas* and the related *Sagas of Icelanders* are key examples of early historical and fictional narrative literature in Europe, and inspired many more modern works, including J.R.R. Tolkein's *The Lord of the Rings*.

An ambitious, educated and wealthy Icelandic Chieftain, Snorri had benefited from the resources of those close to him and made enemies regularly. In parts of the *Eddas*, particularly *The Prose Edda*, Snorri attempts to reconcile the pagan origins of his ancestral folklore with the Christian beliefs that were taking hold across Scandinavia and which he followed. *The Prose Edda* begins with a prologue that is surely the sole creation of Snorri, as it claims 'almighty God created heaven and earth' before referencing Adam and Eve, Noah and the flood, and suggesting that the Norse gods were refugees from Troy.[1] All quite jarring when compared to the rest of *The Prose Edda* and its main sections entitled 'Gylfaginning' – which deals with the creation and destruction of the world – and 'Skaldskaparmal' – in essence a dialogue between the giant Ægir, early Norse personification of the sea, and the god of poetry, Bragi. There are allusions to Loki as occupying an almost proto-Devil role in the *Eddas*, if you go looking for them.

It's once we engage with the main content that we can begin to establish some semblance of who the original

Loki was. Or should I say who Lopt was. Or Loge, or Luk, or...

> 'Loki is pleasing, even beautiful to look at, but his nature is evil and he is undependable. More than others, he has the kind of wisdom known as cunning, and is treacherous in all matters. He constantly places the gods in difficulties and often solves their problems with guile.'[2]

Upon being introduced to Loki in *The Prose Edda*, we're given plenty of warning that this is someone not to be trusted and certainly not to be admired. Norse mythology broadly follows a linear narrative beginning with its creation story and ending (sort of, but not strictly) in the apocalyptic Ragnarök, with a definite plot leading from one event to the next. Our first few experiences of Loki are entertaining and don't present the villain we've been warned to expect. Loki is funny, charming, cunning and deceitful certainly; but driven by boredom as much as anything else, and a trusted companion of Thor and Odin. If we follow the timeline established in the Carnegie Medal-winning author (whose work informed Neil Gaiman's own revision of Norse mythology) Kevin Crossley-Holland's prose retelling of the myths,[3] we enter as witness to Loki the Clown, who does things like take part in a giant's eating contest, steals magical apples to get out of a sticky situation with an eagle, ties a goat to their testicles for some reason, convinces Thor to dress as a bride, and cuts off the goddess Sif's hair in her sleep...

...alright, perhaps there are some red flags.

The turning point comes when Loki tricks the blind god Hod into killing his brother, the much beloved Baldr, during a gathering where the Norse gods are (violently, yet playfully) proving Baldr the Good to be invincible, protected from harm by oaths sworn by almost everything natural and man/god-made. It's unclear why Loki does this – in terms of the story itself, at least, as we can assume that it is designed to serve the broader narrative leading to Loki's siding with the forces of evil during Ragnarök – and certainly *The Prose Edda* offers no real explanation.

The death of Baldr marks a turning point in the characterisation of Loki and in the origin(s) of multiple Loki variations.

In Crossley-Holland's 1980 retelling *The Norse Myths* he depicts Loki as the Sly one; unstable, changing from playful to cruel and heading down a dark path, feeding off the pain and suffering of others.[4] This Sly Loki begrudges Baldr's near imperviousness and is disgusted by the love and delight that Baldr inspires in others. Recounting the legends for a new, younger generation in 2017's illustrated *Norse Myths: Tales of Odin, Thor and Loki*, Crossley-Holland highlights the sordid secrets that Loki knows about many of the other gods – a reference to the poem 'Lokasenna', aka 'Loki's Flyting' or 'Loki's Quarrel'.[5] This supposedly more child-friendly Loki variation is jarred by the spectacle of the gods' revelry in attacking Baldr for fun, knowing what he knows, and increasingly feels contempt for his associates (along with jealously of Baldr's female attention). This is a truly Venomous Loki.

In the d'Aulaires' 1967 *Norse Gods and Giants* (later reprinted as *d'Aulaires' Book of Norse Myths*), which was very clearly intended for children and with delightful, deceptively simplistic illustrations, Loki is identified as God of the Jotun Race (frost giants, and a recurring plot-point in Marvel's many Loki variations). Attractive, articulate and intelligent, the d'Aulaire's Loki has begun to crave attention and affirmation by testing Baldr's invincibility, and prone to fits of rage if he isn't praised for his genius. Jealousy of Baldr's popularity is what gets the better of this Loki, surely serving as an allegorical cautionary tale for young readers prone to hubris.

I could go on citing different examples of how Loki's personality and motivations have been interpreted, such as Neil Gaiman's *Norse Mythology* which closely follows the *Eddas* in offering a Brooding Loki whose mischief has darkened to malice.

Or we could talk about author Joanne Harris's *The Gospel of Loki*, a novel spanning the length of the Norse myths, narrated by Loki in a very contemporary voice. Reading Loki in this way is jarring, almost, to begin with, but comes to make a lot of sense. Harris's *Gospel* Loki is reinterpreted as a fire demon who has escaped from an abstract plain of Chaos and strikes an uneasy alliance with Odin that sees this personification of wildfire become humanised (to some extent at least) and effectively tamed into the role of Trickster of the Gods, so that he may be welcomed into the Norse pantheon. 'Riddled with insecurities' and 'a perpetual outsider',[6] the *Gospel* Loki is written as simultaneously striving for and rebelling against acceptance, dealing with open hostility from gods like Heimdall on a daily basis and having to make increasingly calculated decisions just to survive. Orchestrating the death of Bald(e)r is, for this variation, an act of self-preservation as much as a revenge upon Odin.

Perhaps most unsettling is the Loki variation from A.S. Byatt's novel *Ragnarok: The End of The Gods*, who exhibits qualities and curiosities not unlike a natural scientist. Byatt's Loki seems to engineer the prophesised death of Baldr as some kind of experiment, simply because he can.

Suffice to say that the Baldr incident is frequently referred to and widely recognised as marking a sudden and explicitly villainous change in Loki, though the armchair psychology explanations differ between each retelling.

German literary scholar Stefanie von Schnurbein tried to better understand Loki's motivation for engineering the death of Baldr in a 2000 academic paper, noting that the incident stands out as following the template of a more modern heroic epic.[7] It's possible that Loki performs a function in the *Eddas* of commenting on Norse social hierarchies and sex/gender dynamics of the time, and von Schnurbein supports the assumed Christian influence in Snorri's repackaging of the mythology. We could conclude that in seeking to make the Norse Gods more palatable, some pagan attitudes were rewritten as unnatural or evil, and thus clumsily remade Loki as a stand-in for the devil. This new way of thinking had no room for grey areas; people and deities were either wholly good or wholly bad. Some semblance of this perspective found its way into the first depiction of Loki in a comic book – not the version we recognise today, but a Lucifer-esque Loki in a pink suit, who resides in a fiery pit with various monsters, in *Venus* #6 from 1949.

Part of the problem of who Loki is (and is not), is that there was no cult of Loki during the Viking Age in the same way that prayers and sacrifices were made to Thor, Odin and others; nor did Norse communities feel any kind of imagined benefit from a strong association with Loki, as might have been the case with the siblings Freya and Freyr. Fast-forward to the 21st century and we might view Loki's following rather differently. If we explore the inherent variations in Loki's origins for a wee moment longer, it's important to note that there's very little certainty around what Loki's name actually is and what it means; exactly what kind of deity Loki is and where they came from; and by extension there's little certainty around what we know of Loki's immediate family.

Without a clear and reliable archaeological record to follow, scholars have come up with numerous connections from across European, Asian, and North American cultural traditions to try to determine what Loki's name really is. Depending on who you ask, Loki might be a kind of Scandinavian Prometheus originating in the word logi (fire/flame), or might actually be named Loptr (relating to air), or Lokke/Luki (relating to spiders), or be a God of Closing the Circle/Loop (from the root word lûkan).[8] There are further links, particularly across Scandinavian and Germanic traditions, with demons, goblins, fairies, elves, fireplace spirits, and daddy-long-legs.[9] A broadly popular notion at this point in time is that Loki is connected to knots, tangles or loops in that the god creates tangles in a metaphorical sense (i.e. creates problems), is key to the Ragnarök cycle of death and rebirth, and is credited in Norse mythology with the invention of the fishing net (an event which is itself part of a story in which Loki has caused a tangle in the more socially-problematic way).[10]

I like this latter interpretation of Loki as a God of Knots. Although I'm definitely not an ancient historian, an archaeologist, or an etymologist, I see Loki as a Trickster who occupies a permanently grey area and, while a part of the established pantheon, does not feel genuinely included socially. Tangled up in something they don't necessarily want to be, Loki is mixed up in layers of complexity and uncertainty – both in terms of their narrative and their study.

One striking example of Loki's association with entanglements, from *The Prose Edda*, is in their punishment for the death of Baldr and Baldr's subsequent detention in the Norse underworld, Hel. Having made a getaway while the rest of Asgard was occupied with Baldr's funeral, Loki hides out in a mountain-top house with an entrance on each side (to have full view of anyone coming) and spends much of the daylight hours disguised as a salmon at the bottom of a waterfall. It's during this time that Loki invents the net – which is to be their undoing. A hunting party of gods capture Loki in salmon form, using a net based on Loki's own design, and punish Loki in a rather extreme way.

In a cave, the gods stretched Loki (back in humanoid form) across three large flat stones and bound them to the stones using guts ripped from the body of one of Loki's sons, Narfi (also known as Nari). Narfi's entrails are tied over Loki's shoulders, groin, and knees, before the guts magically transform into iron chains. A snake is fastened above Loki's face and drips poisonous venom towards their face constantly, which Loki's wife Sigyn tries to catch in a bowl. As the bowl periodically filled with venom, Sigyn would have to empty it, thus leaving Loki to endure the poison from time to time. In excruciating pain whenever the snake's poison dripped onto their face, Loki's convulsions would be so violent that they caused earthquakes. Loki was left there in the cave, until the end of all things at Ragnarök.

It's a gruesome scene. Where the reasoning behind Loki's role in the death of Baldr falls short in explaining their turn to evil, Loki's subsequent punishment certainly justifies their position taken alongside monsters, giants, and Hel's armies of the undead during the final battle with the gods at Ragnarök. Perhaps because of the grisly image of Loki's punishment, the scene is played out for several of the Loki variations, though often amended in some way. For example, in Marvel comics miniseries *The Trials of Loki* – which skips the entrails and Sigyn, leaving that Loki to endure a serpent's venom while chained in an almost smiling, Christ-like stance; or in Louie Stowell's hugely entertaining children's book *Loki: A Bad God's Guide to Being Good*, where the disembowelling is again absent but the ever-present threat of a snake dripping poisonous venom onto a Loki-in-child-form is a main driver for much of the plot.[11]

Culture and media scholar Helena Bassil-Morozow highlights physical entrapment as a common feature of trickster narratives across mythology, literature, and cinema,[12] further noting the difficulty in trying to study and pin-down the trickster as a concept. One approach is as a psycho-anthropological metaphor for systemic change in society as a result of an unpredictable, disruptive force. The trickster under restraint may be heroic or destructive, but either way presents a threat to the authority, power, and stability of the status quo. Following Baldr's death, the gods need to bring Loki under control in order to prevent further upset and instability; but the longer Loki is trapped and neglected in the cave, the closer to Ragnarök and seismic change Asgard becomes. The trickster is anti-authoritarian and disrespects social norms, crossing boundaries and breaking taboos, and so the status quo hinges on whether the trickster can be tamed.[13]

In another, earlier instance, the *Eddas* Loki breaks with social convention by cheating their way out of losing a bet. In recompense for cutting off Sif's hair (and to avoid being beaten to near-death by Thor), Loki commissions

20

two dwarf brothers to forge great treasures for the gods, including golden hair for Sif, but wagers that the brothers can't make each treasure equally as grand. If they in fact can, Loki bets, then the dwarves could take Loki's head. Inevitably, events transpire whereby Loki has to evade losing their head to the brothers Brokk and Eitri; and argues that the dwarves are entitled to Loki's head but have no right to harm their neck. Failing to reach agreement over where Loki's head ended and neck began, Brokk stitched Loki's lips together in frustration instead.

The trickster is either representative of a primitive, shameless creature, or a brave challenge to the system; whatever our perspective, in the eyes of the establishment the trickster must face restriction as punishment for rule-breaking. But within every definition of Loki falls multiple interpretations: good, bad, humourous, virtuous, evil; a mass to untangle, a knotted character. It all depends on your point of view and whose rules the trickster is in breach of. Did the rest of the Norse pantheon deserve to be taken down a peg or two, every now and then? Where did Loki actually come from and where did their allegiance truly lie? Perhaps we ought to exist in the grey areas, like Loki, rather than see everything in black and white.

Within every variation are knots to untangle, and even with persistence, we may never be done.

Chapter 2
God of Mischief

The sheer number of Marvel variations we could explore would realistically take up a book all of their own, if we were to try to pick apart every scheme, plot, ploy, jape, hoodwink, and nefarious plan of the numerous comic book interpretations we're all at least a little familiar with. As before, Loki was not, originally, the God of Mischief. Mischievous, certainly, but not a title that the naughty/knotty deity was bestowed with back in ancient mythological times. Over the last decade plus, Marvel's MCU, though not the first to explore this side of Loki, have cemented the God of Mischief moniker through actor Tom Hiddleston's portrayal, marking him as our contemporary status quo Loki variation.

Hiddleston's MCU Loki is intelligent, charming and fragile, with a need for validation that bubbles furiously under the surface of his smile. I find it hard to differentiate between the actor's performance and the character as written, in trying to locate the source of the MCU Loki's Byronesque qualities; the self-destructive romanticism that surrounds this Loki and his journey is a core component in this variation's appeal. Family is another key aspect of the MCU Loki; the relationships between Loki, Thor, Odin, Frigga, and Hela are what drive much of the main narrative across the *Thor* movies and *Loki* TV show. It's part of what underpins the Loki variations across Marvel media, but particularly with the MCU Loki, the need to be acknowledged and appreciated by those closest to him.

Across the *Eddas*, Loki is essentially a blood-brother to Odin, and a confidant and travelling companion to Thor. In Snorri's *Prose Edda*, Loki's father is a male jotun/jötunn named Fárbauti and his mother is called Laufey or Nál (though it's unclear exactly who or what she is). However, when writer Stan Lee and artist Jack Kirby introduced what would later become known as Marvel's Classic Loki in 1962's *Journey Into Mystery* #111, they almost immediately established ongoing family strife in the Thor comics by diverting from mythology to make Loki 'The God of Mischief', the brother and 'sworn enemy' of Thor, and both of them the sons of Odin.[1] Comic writer Keiron Gillen puts it succinctly thus '…he was a manipulative creature born of jealousy'.[2]

Over the course of the 1960s, Classic Loki makes various ill-fated attempts at ruling Asgard (home of Marvel's Norse pantheon), defeating Thor or taking his magical hammer Mjolnir, to varying degrees of outland-ishness. These include: using illusions and mind control (for example with The Hulk in 1963's *Avengers* #1); shape-shifting and disguises (it's unclear why Classic Loki needs disguises, when he can transform into other people and animals); aiding in the creation and/or release of other villains (including the Fire Demon Surtur); using Thor's romantic interest Jane Foster in some way, and; more than once, getting Thor mixed-up in the Vietnam War.

Obviously.

The ongoing brotherly conflict meant that Thor would never use excessive (in relative comic book terms) force against Loki and instead leave the door open for him to return to cause trouble in a later issue; while as the simul-taneously doting and hard-line father, Odin could find an excuse to either intervene or merely observe whatever villainous scheme his openly less-favoured son had afoot. When the comics later reveal and revise Loki to in fact be the child of Frost Giants (with his regal birthfather taking the name of Laufey, here), adopted into the Asgardian royalty, it others him and distances his monstrousness and wickedness from the assumed nobility and right-eousness of Thor and Odin. Fast forward to Kenneth Branagh's Shakespearean blockbuster *Thor* (2011) and this Adopted Other plot point is repeated as the means by which Loki as troublemaker becomes Loki as villain, hurt and lashing out against his surrogate family.

However, the larger arc of Hiddleston's MCU Loki is one of redemption, in an almost opposite direction of travel from the *Eddas* Loki. In the mythology, Loki will ultimately lead the forces of evil to Ragnarök, the end of all things; whereas in the MCU's *Thor: Ragnarok* (2017) the God of Mischief will stand alongside other heroes to protect lives when the end of Asgard is upon them, and play a key role in defeating the real villain of the piece. Throughout the MCU's episodic story, Thor, played by Chris Hemsworth, holds on to the belief that his adopted brother retains some sense of good and selflessness in him, despite his claims to the contrary. Appeals are made to this Loki's better nature time and again, whether in sparing the people of a small town in New Mexico in *Thor* (2011), coming home from exile in *Avengers* (2012), or avenging the murder of their mother Frigga in *Thor: The Dark World* (2013).

Hiddleston got the opportunity to take the character in a slightly different direction in the first season of the television show *Loki* (2021) on the Disney+ streaming platform. Initially identifying himself as a villain, the MCU Loki's facade drops as his future is revealed to him – a life cut short having failed to achieve his dreams of rule – and he admits that his cruelty and harm are an extreme form of self-preservation rather than a purely evil nature. The show develops the MCU variation as a kind of anti-hero as the god's perspective is broadened and faced with powers and problems more important than he will ever be. His self-interest, a driving force in many of his actions, is fuelled by the emergence of his own dimensional doppelgangers, with the show's narrative repeatedly returning to the theme of self-discovery, that in turn leads the MCU Loki to display leadership and compassion for others. The seeds of this compassion were already there, back in 2011 when this attractive and charming variation first graced our screens. An emotionally layered character, the MCU Loki is the villain of the first *Thor* installment and yet remains affectionate and deferential to his adoptive mother, Frigga.

Not by coincidence, 2011 also saw a new Loki in Marvel's comics, as the old *Journey Into Mystery* title was reinstated for writer Gillen to tell the story of the God of Mischief resurrected with the body of a child and a need to make amends for past behaviour. This kind of media synergy has become almost standard practice for the comic book movies of the 21st century – revamping a character or comic that has a film adaptation about to be released. Media scholar Henry Jenkins has described this as transmedia storytelling; the process(es) by which different forms of media deliver different components of a piece of fiction, where each component (e.g. a movie, an in-universe role-play game, a comic telling a prequel story, a colouring book using key characters/scenes) is unique and can be enjoyed individually, but when consumed altogether the components offer a complete and interconnected whole cultural product.[3] Jenkins has offered several examples of the wider fictional universes that utilise transmedia storytelling, including *The Matrix*, *Pokémon*, *Doctor Who*, *Star Wars*, and Marvel and DC comics, as he has sought to refine his notion of convergence culture in the face of standard academic nit-picking and pedantry.[4]

Hiddleston has described himself as a 'temporary torchbearer' in playing the MCU Loki[5] – who is but one of several Loki variations among the wider Marvel output of films and television, games and toys, books and of course, comics spanning over sixty years. Separate from this decades-long franchising as a business approach to media production, and yet often an in-built artistic/editorial decision, transmedia storytelling content is intended to aid in world-building and establishing backstory, and in exploring the actions and experiences of other characters relevant to the central plot. Serialised fiction, such as the MCU and the Marvel comics (which are intended to be read as over sixty years' worth of a single but expansive, continuous narrative)[6] is particularly well-suited to transmedia as a means of engaging audiences more deeply and passionately.

The events of the MCU movies can be enjoyed individually or as part of an ongoing saga, as can the tie-in books and guides, or the *Loki* (2021) and animated *What If?* (2021) series, but when these are all consumed as a full story centred around core, returning characters, audiences have access to a more immersive, interactive, and hopefully elevated form of cultural entertainment. Certainly, the Marvel fandom would seem to agree, if the global financial success of the MCU is anything to go by.

And I haven't even mentioned fan-fiction yet.

What I want to propose here is that Marvel's innate skill with transmedia storytelling has directly contributed to the successful redemption of its Loki variations in the 21st century, from villains to anti-heroes – both on screen and in the comics. As one handsome variation was gaining a fan-following on the big screen, another variation was offering something new and just as engaging in the pages of the Marvel comics.

Kid Loki was introduced as the sort-of reincarnation of the God of Mischief, a child with some but not all of the same powers and personality traits (and accompanied by a magpie with the spirit of his former, older self), following him sacrificing himself to save a new Asgard (floating above Oklahoma) from an escalating siege that he had engineered in the first place…

Comics, honestly…

Introduced by writer Matt Fraction, but expanded upon and more commonly associated with Gillen, Kid Loki marked the beginning of the character's journey away from decades as a malevolent Prince of Evil towards someone more complex, thoughtful, empathetic, and unpredictable. This young godling was an opportunity to explore why Thor doesn't simply kill his evil adopted brother and end his reign of terror, as Kid Loki looks to Thor for support and understanding, in his (apparent) attempts to go straight and atone for his past. Indeed, Kid Loki's feelings towards Thor were genuinely loving, in a way that would never have been possible with the original villainous incarnation. Befitting its loose Norse mythology influences, this revamped *Journey Into Mystery* series could use Kid Loki to discuss the ideas of fate and human (godly?) nature, and the grey areas between good and evil.

Kid Loki proved popular with readers of *Thor* and *Journey Into Mystery* and soon found his way into other Marvel comic titles, including *New Mutants* and *Young Avengers*. A live-action Kid Loki (played by Jack Veal) would go on to appear in episode 5 of *Loki* season 1, alongside appearances of other variations Sylvie (Sophia Di Martino), Classic Loki (Richard E. Grant), Boastful Loki (DeObia Oparei), President Loki (Hiddleston pulling a double-shift), and a CGI Alligator Loki. The title of that episode was, appropriately, 'Journey Into Mystery'.

While the child god was not entirely a good person, nor a straightforward hero, the redemption of Loki in Marvel comics continued at a steady pace and sought to capitalise on the appeal of a young, attractive God of Mischief as seen on screen, by having Kid Loki age a wee bit up to appear roughly in his late teens/early twenties in the *Loki: Agent of Asgard* comic series that followed. Here, Loki is more explicitly seeking to be a better version of himself and contribute in a positive (though, secret) way to his Asgardian community. From here, the Marvel comics variation(s) continues to walk a redemptive path, more or less. Indeed, recently Al Ewing, the writer of *Loki: Agent of Asgard*, said, 'I don't think you'll get a story with Loki as an out-and-out baddie for a long time'.[7]

During the *Agent of Asgard* period (2014–2015) Ewing has his *Agent* Loki variation casually change gender on a couple of occasions, and in *Original Sin* #5.5 (a comic that tied-in to an event storyline across several titles) Odin refers to his children 'My son (Thor) and my daughter (Angela – a recent addition) and my child who is both (Loki)'.[8] This wasn't a revelatory happening, either, as during J. Michael Straczynski's run writing *Thor* comics over five years earlier, Loki had returned to the forefront in the guise of Lady Loki (possessing the body of fellow Asgardian Lady Sif), though this was really little more than a gimmick for about a year.

Roughly fifteen years on from Lady Loki, Marvel comics' Loki is now broadly recognised as being canonically genderfluid and bisexual or pansexual (depending on the writer),[9] and Hiddleston's MCU Loki has made tentative steps in the same direction. The 21st century has seen a progressive change in mainstream superhero-dominated comics, seeking to correct decades of under-representation by explicitly engaging with intersections of class, sex and gender, race and ethnicity, sexuality, and disability.[10] Heroes like Northstar, Wiccan, Hulkling, and America Chavez are prominent queer characters in Marvel comics, while Batwoman, Renee Montoya, and Aqualad lead LGBTQ+ representation in DC comics.

Now, that's not to suggest that diversity and representation are matters that have been solved in comics by any means – there are complex backstories to what comics creators have achieved up to this point, and caveats abound. What is interesting (to me, at least) is that, as academic endeavours, queer theory and comics theory share similar characteristics. Professor of American Cultural Studies Daniel Stein explains that both are 'an amalgamation of perspectives from various disciplines rather than a unified approach', and partly explore shifting cultural trends and multi-layered signs/codes in popular culture.[11]

*

Historically a pejorative and still contested in some arenas today, queer has been gradually reclaimed in everyday life over the last thirty or so years as a self-reflexive, self-constructed and potentially fluid distinction.[12] Fundamental to being queer is to exist outwith the inherently strict definitions of heteronormativity and be inclusive of millions of people whose sense of who they are and how they live their lives are not reduced to being (one might say merely) a straight, cis male or female. Covering a spectrum of sex, gender, and desire is not intended to replace the hard-fought identities under the LGBTQ+ umbrella, but rather to offer an optional broadening of how these identities are understood and expressed.[13]

As an academic pursuit, queer theory seeks to explore, explain, and embrace the contradictions and category resistance involved in rejecting essentialist, or supposedly natural, definitions and expectations of sex, gender, and desire. Queer theory was established as something of an academic mosaic (associated to varying degrees with scholars including Judith Butler, Eve Kosofsky Sedgwick, and Michael Warner) in the 1990s, sharing elements of postmodern, post-structuralist critical thinking and a variety of analytical approaches that may be used to challenge dominant and fixed discourses around identity, social issues, politics, culture, theology and more.[14]

Queer studies scholar Annamarie Jagose discusses how problematising previously accepted 'logical' claims of identity categories, and increasingly recognising the complexity of how our personal sense of who we are is formed both by and against the dominant symbolic codes and myths of everyday life, has been a positive step in advancing science and social theory.[15]

On a superficial level, the Marvel variations of Loki are set apart from the heteronormative, hypermasculine ideal of Thor(s): typically leaner and less statuesque than most other Asgardians, who tend to reinforce a rigidity in both appearance and demeanour; with less oversized muscle mass allowing for greater flexibility and expression in Loki's body language. There is a suggestion of physical weakness and fragility. To make Marvel's Loki variations more conspicuous in their otherness or unmanliness, they're traditionally dressed in garish, theatrical green and yellow/gold outfits – particularly in some of the more classic comics drawn by Jack Kirby, John Buscema, Walt Simonson and others.

We should also address the matter of the Marvel variations' bizarre and intrusive curved-horn helmets. Seemingly a deliberate aesthetic choice, this imagery has been found on a handful of remaining 10th century stone carvings, depicting the Norse God from a more Christian perspective of evil and deviancy.

From Norse oral tradition to the Christian-era retelling, and on into Marvel comics, Loki as a norm-challenging trickster who critiques hypermasculinity will always be read as deviant. What matters is how we interpret the word 'deviant' and, tragically, in Western society we tend to find deviancy negatively conflated with queer. Fictional villains and anti-heroes have often been read by fans as queer, or occasionally were intentionally written as queer; either way, queer-coding in popular culture can be problematic if mishandled.[16] Actions that don't conform to the espoused norms and values of the vocal majority in society have been labelled as deviancy, historically. Social scientists have studied the negative, and often harmful or even criminalised responses to people whose appearance and/or behaviour were deemed socially unacceptable or transgressive; and the notions of taboos, moral boundaries, and conformity as social regulators.

But the trickster, as a mythical figure as well as in contemporary fiction, is supposed to be transgressive! The aforementioned Helena Bassil-Morozow reminds us tricksters are intended to push boundaries and challenge taboos, whether in their flouting of sex and gender binaries, dominant narratives around acceptable sexualities, or in their shapeshifting and lack of a single, category-pleasing sense of self.[17] Lady Loki in Straczynski's Marvel comics, the Sylvie Variant in the *Loki* series on Disney+, *Agent of*

Asgard Loki's gender fluidity, Classic Loki's transformations into various birds, snakes and whatnot in the early comics, Hiddleston's MCU Loki's abilities of illusion projection and duplication – all take their cue from the queer-coded shapeshifting of the original *Eddas* Loki.

Let's revisit the opening line about how I'll never see Tom Hiddleston shapeshift into a mare to have sex with a giant's horse and birth a mythological creature. The *Eddas* Loki voluntarily transformed into a female horse in order to seduce and lure a giant stonemason's stallion away into the night. As Snorri recounts '…Loki's relations with [the horse] were such that a while later he [sic] gave birth to a colt'.[18] The *Eddas* Loki births the great eight-legged horse Sleipnir – who becomes the All-Father Odin's trusty steed – and this is more or less an average day for them. In addition, Loki has two sons with their wife Sigyn; and fathers the Midgard Serpent Jörmungandr, the giant wolf Fenrir, and Hel (goddess of the underworld), with the ogress (or female jotun/jötunn, both giant races are attributed) Angrboda/Angrboða.

While these associations and activities are watered down considerably in Marvel properties, what remains are the perceived otherworldly or un-godly nature of Loki's relationships – often frowned-upon or derided by their peers. Loki is therefore othered even within the Norse pantheon, emphasising how subversive their lifestyle is viewed in comparison to everyone else.

To borrow someone else's headline, Loki was always queer.[19] This was embraced by author Mackenzi Lee when Marvel hired her to write the young adult novel *Loki: Where Mischief Lies*, in which a young Loki wrestles with his feelings of being an outsider and a disappointment among his family. From the moment the novel was announced, Lee was clear that it would read Loki as canonically queer and offer LGBTQ+ representation.[20]

Lee's high-heel wearing Loki is already tired of trying to find acceptance in Asgard and becoming increasingly reliant on the understanding and encouragement of his mother Frigga and friend Amora, the Enchantress. A prophecy implying Loki will lead an army against Asgard paints him as a problem, an embarrassment for his father, one that needs to be brought in line with more noble and mainstream expectations. Subsequently exiled in Victorian London, Lee's Loki is not so much trying to come out; it's clarified later in the novel that reductive and restraining binaries of sex, gender and sexuality simply don't exist on Asgard (which must be nice), but rather is trying to work out who he's coming out as. The historical backdrop provides deliberately chosen context in which to read Loki's exploration of who he is becoming versus who he is judged as. Whether trying to find the words to describe his feelings towards Amora and Theo (a young man he meets in London) or investigating the source (internal or external?) of his powers, Lee's Loki is seeking to reconcile being a prince, a witch, and a God of Chaos all at the same time. That this Loki variation is both openly and subtextually queer is most pleasing.

The Marvel variations of Loki cause mayhem and destruction as an almost primal instinct to feel belonging, and inevitably return to questions of their own identity, and of how others see them. A God of Mischief and reactionary rebellion, certainly, but also a young man seeking attention and acceptance; the Marvel variations have slowly but significantly contributed to the normalisation of queer characters in pop culture. Across various media and medium, the 21st century's most popular trickster is (ironically enough) increasingly a stand-in for people who feel overlooked, vilified, or who are apparently on the outside of mainstream society. Whatever mainstream is supposed to mean these days.

If Loki speaks for the Others, the Outsiders, then we need to better understand who these people are, and acknowledge that many, if not all the variations are themselves outcasts.

Chapter 3
God of Outcasts

Even now, in the 21st century when there has never been a greater diversity of people and celebration of our differences as individuals, there remain stigmas and stereotypes, and domination and persecution of one group by another, in all walks of everyday life. Such is human nature, and it would seem, godly nature too. It stands to reason – we must have learnt it from somewhere. People still label their peers as freaks, deviants, perverts, weirdos, losers, and more besides. For many, acts and attitudes that appear resistant to the status quo, or that subvert mainstream ideas and behaviours, can still appear as threatening.

In the *Eddas*, Loki is treated similarly, and this has informed how many of their variations have been imbued with elements that resonate with many of us to this day. Verbally attacked by other Norse gods in the Eddic poem 'Lokasenna', Loki is clearly seen as untrustworthy and unnatural. Their shapeshifting, relationships, and birthing of several children of various forms are all judged in negative terms, and Loki's allegiance is questioned as a result. Granted, some of this questioning is justified given the god's history of causing almost as much trouble as they help resolve.

The *Eddas* Loki gives as good as they get in 'Lokasenna' but as the novel *The Gospel of Loki* by Joanne Harris evidences time and again, Loki's origins and perspective on life, the universe, and everything will forever see the god be treated as an outcast. A fire demon from Chaos itself, Harris's *Gospel* Loki is surprisingly self-aware although his narration cannot be entirely trusted. Beginning the novel as the personification of wildfire, the *Gospel* Loki already feels like unpredictability and living without boundaries are fundamental parts of his nature. He recognises that his curiosity about exploring the Nine Worlds makes him somewhat 'perverse' in comparison to his fellow Chaos demons and is fully aware of how unwelcome he is in Asgard too, when Odin convinces him to join their ranks of well-dressed and morally-superior gods.

Throughout the novel, this Loki variation faces a kind of xenophobia complete with threats of violence, micro-aggressions, social exclusion, and distrust. His openness regarding his views on the constraints of heter-onormative monogamy, and the hypocrisy of many of the Norse gods in relation to this, is one of a number of issues where the pantheon finds the *Gospel* Loki's position obscene. Heimdall, the Watchman or the Guardian of the Rainbow Bridge Bifröst, has a particular hatred of the *Gospel* Loki from the moment he arrives in Asgard until their fight to the death(ish) at Ragnarök. The Watchman calls this variation 'revolting' for birthing the horse Sleipnir, and later degrades the *Gospel* Loki as inhabiting a 'miserable life'.[1]

In *The Gospel of Loki*, Heimdall (along with Thor, Tyr, Sif, and others) is effectively an enforcer for the unwritten social rules governing Asgardian behaviour in public. Everyday norms and values vary by culture and community, and are social constructions informed by relationships of power and archaic notions of what is good and right vs what is evil and wrong. A classic text on understanding deviance as a socially-imposed label, rather than an inherent trait and pathology, *Outsiders* by the sociologist Howard Becker highlights the control that isolating (or even imprisoning) those who are different as deviant exerts over society, and the inequalities of power it justifies.[2] Having come to Asgard from another plain of existence where the culture is vastly different, the *Gospel* Loki is instantly singled out as being an outsider and is never fully accepted as an equal by the Norse gods (not

even his blood-brother Odin). The victimising and vili-
fying of this Loki for not fitting neatly into the rules of
acceptable behaviour performs two simultaneous func-
tions: the *Gospel* Loki is singled-out as deviating from the
assumed norm, and his treatment by the social enforcers
sends a clear message to the rest of the gods to fear him and
consciously avoid being branded as deviant themselves.

The fundamentals of this kind of experience, being cast
out or feeling on the outside, will be known to many
of us, and from an early age. It's no coincidence that
many Loki variations view reality through the eyes of the
young; for example in Marvel's pre-teen Kid Loki, the
assumed teenager in Diana Wynne Jones's novel *Eight
Days of Luke*, the god trapped in the body of an eleven-
year-old in Louie Stowell's *Loki: A Bad God's Guide To...*
book series, and the Norwegian Netflix series *Ragnarok*.

A teen drama that is slightly confused between Norse
mythology and Marvel comics, *Ragnarok* sees Magne and
his younger brother Laurits return to the town of their
birth, only to uncover that they and most of the other
main characters are either the enduring or reincarnated
figures from the Norse pantheon and their giant antago-
nists. Magne is sort-of Thor, Laurits is sort-of Loki, and
the ever-present threats of climate change and battling
the local wealthy (evil) family are the sort-of impending
Ragnarok.

Having the Loki variation of *Ragnarok* be a sardonic teenager going through an identity crisis, while feeling held back in his small town and superior to his brother, is actually an almost perfect set-up. Played by Jonas Strand Gravli, the seventeen-year-old Laurits carries the kind of cheeky charisma, brooding, and bubbling emotion that one would hope for in a Loki variation, with genuine unpredictability. That Laurits's own subplots see him contend with a revelation about his parentage, and coming out, also ring true. The part about the tapeworm (no spoilers on that one), not so much.

In a key scene between Laurits and his mother, early in Season 2, Laurits feels foolish after waiting for his crush to arrive at a house party. The young man never turns up, causing Laurits to pine for some sense of companionship and belonging – something he's never truly felt within his immediate family. Obviously, this is the perfect moment for his slightly-inebriated mother to reveal that his father was not who he thought he was – but is in fact the patriarch of the villainous local family of sort-of giants, making Magne his half-brother. A tale as old as time. The character of Laurits is partly a representation of the feelings of being an outsider or a 'freak' (as he describes himself) that young people often struggle with because of having internalised the ignorance and pre-judice of others, sometimes accompanied by forms of self-doubt or even self-hate. Being queer in a small town would be enough on its own, in this respect, but this Loki variation also has to contend with what is viewed as the illegitimacy of his birth.

In fiction and lore, as in life, people are categorised and measured against normative standards during social interaction. Here certain personal attributes may come to light which are deemed unattractive, discrediting or deviant by those outside of one's usual social group; or which do not fit within general societal norms.[3] Stigmas, stereotypes, and prejudices are born in such circumstances. In the case of popular culture, stigma may be applicable to an entire medium, damaging both the cultural object and people associated with it.

During the 1950s, as McCarthyism swept the USA, the efforts of one phsychiatrist and author Dr. Frederic Wertham fuelled moral panic regarding imagined delinquency and sexual deviancy in children reading comics. The institutional self-censoring established by fearful publishers resulted in comics aimed at adults being largely forced underground. This censorship contributed to the stigma of comics and associated pop culture genres such as science fiction and fantasy being perceived as discredited cultural forms, resulting in negative attitudes towards adult pop culture fans for much of the 20th century – personified in the stereotype of the 'fanboy'.[4]

This stigmatisation of popular culture, particularly in comic-adjacent works for adults, was largely a Western phenomenon, however; in Japan the Manga style of comics have been incredibly popular for well over a century.[5] *The Mythical Detective Loki Ragnarok* by manga artist Sakura Kinoshita was published from 1999 – 2004 and adapted as a television anime (as manga often are). Here, Loki has been cast out of Asgard by a furious Odin and hides out in Tokyo, setting up a detective agency to help him work out why he's been exiled and why various other Norse gods keep popping up to try and kill him. In manga's distinctive black and white art style, this *Mythical Detective* Loki has also been trapped in the form of a young boy, which doesn't seem to be too much of a barrier in collecting the evil forces he encounters in his investigations. It's all somehow very far from the *Eddas* and yet maintained a dedication to them. Besides the distinctive art style and some more common manga tropes, this variation isn't that far removed from any other Loki we might encounter – it's just a very different set of circumstances he finds himself in.

In this case, the Loki variation is an outcast for the purposes of an entertaining plot. In some other variations, the outcast is the platform or the medium by which that Loki is encountered, as was the case for the Western superhero comics and associated pop culture forms that were discredited for much of the 20th century. And in further examples, the outcasts are the audience themselves – the fans from our own reality.

Today, fandoms are more numerous and visible than ever, establishing physical and virtual communities around the world and uniting people from all walks of life. Research continues to grow and diversify to keep up with all the branches of fans, subcultures, audiences, and neo-tribes that can be identified by their shared consumption and celebration of particular cultural forms – whether it be comics, football, a music genre, an actor, a board game, a book series, or beyond.

Media scholar Henry Jenkins explains how fandoms, as a form of cultural solidarity, afford consumers identities within social communities which are defined purely by their relationship with, and expertise in, specific texts and artefacts (e.g., comics or cult television series).[6] What they broadly share is their organisation around practices and degrees of consumption; meaning that casual fans can share spaces and interact with more die-hard fans (though they don't always have/want to) and individuals commonly move among separate and related fandoms as they wish. A fan might display their allegiance by wearing their team colours, or homemade cosplay of their favourite fictional character; they might cheer a goal scored as they sit in a stadium, or cheer a trailer debuted in a convention hall. It's still only relatively recently, with the increased mainstreaming (and therefore profiting) of many forms and genres within pop culture, that their associated fans have become more included and celebrated in everyday life.[7] In the past, fans of comic books, fantasy and science fiction were infantilised, labelled as obsessive and degenerate, pathologised, bullied, and more. Indeed, during the 1980s a moral panic swept across parents of teenagers who enjoyed the role-playing table-top game *Dungeons and Dragons*. Young people who already felt like social pariahs in their schools and neighbourhoods were accused of engaging in the occult when they rolled their many-sided dice and welcomed demons into their homes.

While the suggestion that fandoms are comparable to religions or cults in not a new one, the concern is more whether this comparison is seen in (relatively) objective terms or is itself negatively and harmfully viewed, or perhaps even disrespectful and blasphemous. We could perhaps sidestep such problematic perspectives by instead likening the devotion of fans to being similar to sacred experiences,[8] or as falling somewhere between cult, community, and culture as a form of neo-religiosity.[9]

Despite not having a cult following during the Viking Age – or at least not to anything like the same extent that Odin, Thor, and some other Norse gods did – we're certainly making up for it now in the mass production of Loki idols. In terms of Marvel and MCU Loki variations, there appear to have been thirty separate Loki Funko Pop collectable bobble-head designs manufactured so far. You'll very likely have seen these figures with their distinctive oversized heads and black circles for eyes on colleagues' desks and in friends' homes – if not your own. Full disclosure: I have two.

The Digital Age has allowed for the global expansion of the 21st century following of Loki. There are, for example, over 21 billion views of #loki videos on TikTok at the time of writing, with many more millions across respective Loki tag offshoots, most of which showcase Hiddleston's Loki in various situations and edits capturing the many facets of the fandom. There are also approaching 450,000 Tumblr followers of #loki – the majority of which link to blogs focused on the MCU Loki and Hiddleston, posting and sharing gifs and fanart on a regular basis. Some explanation for this following may be divined from the typically romantic and/or explicit content of much MCU Loki fanart and fanfiction, featuring a relationship between Loki and Thor, or between Loki and Sylvie or Mobius from the TV show, or with the author/reader themselves. The beautiful, but dark and mysterious queer outsider deity is apparently quite an appealing type.

*

The dedicated followers of long-running fantasy drama *Supernatural* are no strangers to fanfiction either, having established the 'Wincest' genre in which the lead characters Dean and Sam Winchester are written as having incestuous affairs (over 11,000 Archive of Our Own fan-stories appear in the 'Wincest' search alone, to show the scale of investment). Over the course of the fifteen seasons of the show, the *Supernatural* fandom has almost become a phenomenon of its own and often influenced the course of the show (there's literally an episode called 'Fan Fiction', full of references and mockery of earlier episodes).

Supernatural's Loki variation is commonly referred to as the Trickster for the first five seasons, played by Richard Speight Jr. Leaning into a more conventional interpretation of the character, with this variation often enjoying playing deadly games with a kind of 'gallows humour'; the Trickster creates illusions and elaborate scenarios for fun. Examples include trapping the Winchester brothers in a time loop, and later a television reality, to try to prove a point on both occasions. Distrustful of authority (usually literal Higher Powers), the Trickster is often encountered amid a scheme to take someone important down a peg without exposing his true identity. He's later forced to reveal that he is in fact the Archangel Gabriel, and later still he explains that he had struck a deal with the real Loki (while releasing him from his bindings in a cave…) to take his identity in a form of 'witness protection'. Having sent himself into exile to evade his dysfunctional family and their heavenly conflict, the Trickster/Gabriel recognises that he himself is an outcast despite his incredible position, unable to find belonging among his peers and searching for a new purpose. Several overarching plot threads relate to the Trickster/Gabriel over the course of *Supernatural*, as the wider mythology established in the show itself takes precedent over ties to lore established in our own reality.

What's interesting about the Trickster/Gabriel is that he's written and played as a character closer to what we might expect of a Loki variation – with a dark but playful sense of humour, the abilities to change appearance and create projections, and a theatricality in actions like clicking his fingers to signal using his powers – that the 'real' Loki of *Supernatural* does not evidence at all. Indeed, the evocative sewing of Loki's lips from Norse mythology is a punishment handed out to the Trickster/Gabriel, instead. Personality-wise, Gabriel is often accused of being cowardly (which he counters with bravado) while the *Supernatural* Loki harbours more of the resentment and anger seen in the *Eddas* Loki as they get closer to Ragnarök. The effect, intended or not, is an interesting juxtaposition between the two Loki variations (played by the same actor) in the one show, both outcasts in their own differing ways.

The Trickster/Gabriel has exiled himself from Heaven to escape the Apocalypse and as result is ostracised (as well as hunted) by his father and Archangel brothers. *Supernatural*'s 'true' Loki has been banished and imprisoned by his father and maintains a low profile upon his release. Neither demigod wants to be discovered by their peers, nor would they be welcomed back into their respective families without always being known as the black sheep, the outcast.

A more literal example of a variation as an outcast is established towards the end of the Marvel comic *Loki: The God Who Fell to Earth*, written by Daniel Kibblesmith – in which the reborn Trickster has learned the valuable lesson in warmongering not to get caught. This miniseries finds its Loki imprisoned in a supermax prison and being questioned by perhaps his only friend in the universe. Kibblesmith's Loki is reflecting on the truth of his own memories and whether he can trust the way he remembers his life and rebirths up to this point. Over the course of his existence in the comics, the Marvel variations have taken a long, winding journey from being the God of Evil, then Lies, then Mischief, to more recently the God of Stories. While Kibblesmith's Loki is unclear on the accuracy of the past, present and future that he claims to see all at once for himself, he does know that he can rely on his recollections of being repeatedly excluded and/or expelled from society.

This variation avoids reflecting too deeply on his own blame for much of this, but he has clearly been hurt time and again when his actions have led to him being cast out of 'kingdoms... families... [and] universes'.[10] With no-one else to rely on, nor a place to call home, he declares:

'I am Loki. God of Outcasts. They see themselves in me. And I in them. All of us. Alone together.'[11]

Since Tom Hiddleston's MCU Loki has found popularity with his variation and his ongoing tension between rebellion and compassion, so too have the wider Marvel variations gained layers of complexity and sympathy in their characterisations. Openly admitting to having been directly influenced by Kibblesmith's Loki,[12] the Director and Executive Producer of *Loki*'s first season, Kate Herron, had Richard E. Grant's Classic Loki variation use the moniker God of Outcasts in the 'Journey Into Mystery' episode the following year (adding another small but specific detail to Marvel's intertextual web). Grant's Classic Loki has also been reflecting on his past and has arrived at the conclusion that everywhere he goes, he brings pain to himself and those around him.

His solution is to fake his death and live in total seclusion, ultimately proving himself right when loneliness gets the better of him and upon being discovered, Grant's Classic Loki is banished to a kind of purgatory.

These Marvel variations are tapping into what I see as a plurality in the reading of Loki as the God of Outcasts: as being a patron saint of outsiders, or personification of the feeling of otherness, and in being an idol whose following is composed of such people.

The variations in this chapter have equated Loki with being a deviant outsider, an unwanted freak, a fallen angel estranged from their family, and someone who may well be better off in exile from the rest of society. Relatedly, we've also touched on the contemporary followers of Loki themselves and how the forms in which they engage with Loki may associate them with being seen as outcasts. Understanding why someone is made an outcast (or feels forced to exclude themselves) is in fact an exercise in understanding where the concepts of right and wrong, and of what is acceptable in civilised society, have come from. In Asgard, as in our own reality, norms and values are the reserve of the homogeneous mass population. Such a distribution of power is unfair and not at all representative – by deliberate and enduring design – of the diversity of peoples, pursuits, and ideas in everyday life.

The God of Outcasts role that Loki plays in many variations is an outsider that we can identify with and escape to. Someone who struggles against the same fundamental prejudice and exclusion that we may be going through, and more often than not, Loki prevails. Loki wins the day and we can escape into the variations to share in their triumphs, but with the knowledge that tomorrow it might be something else. A fantasy perhaps, but still a grounded one.

It's in the celebrating or even the idolising of the outsider that we have a moment to feel welcome and part of an alternative community. Fandoms, for example, are their own societal microcosms where those who may have once felt isolated can find belonging. Everyone can be a fan of something and more often than not are fans of several things at once. The standards expected within fandoms are more reflective of the identities and interests that they include. It's not always a perfect utopia, but it's certainly much more aware of how power imbalances manifest and maintain themselves.[13] The labours of fans in creating art and fiction inspired by pop culture are subversive acts in their own right; resisting and destabilising the protected status quo of corporate copyright and intellectual property, in the pursuit of personal expression, inclusion, and acceptance.[14]

Chapter 4
God of Stories

We can quite reliably describe all the Loki variations as fanfiction. All the variations are adaptations of original folkloric canon shared via oral tradition, and are works that have been interpreted, amended, and personalised (sometimes politicised) by their creators – whether historian, fiction writer, comic book artist, or film director. As I've said, all the Loki variations are legitimate because each one is somebody's Loki.

They're all just stories. So, if Loki is the God of Stories, then what kind of stories are we using them to tell?

As we explore who Loki is and who some of their variations are, we inevitably unpack the social, political and cultural subtexts that have informed how these variations are constructed. Some are more deliberate than others, but what every variation shares is a creator whose own thoughts and feelings have (to varying extents) found their way into the writing and world-building of that narrative. Fiction can be a powerful tool by which to explore themes and issues that are pertinent to our own lived realities – this has always been the case. In recent years there have been increasing examples of the arts and social sciences coming together in the form of sociological fiction;[1] disseminating fields of research and their findings via creative writing either instead of, or accompanying, the more traditional academic thesis or monograph.

This isn't really a new idea, though, to explain the world through stories. The skalds of the Viking Age were poets who composed ornate works intended to commu-nicate current events, battles, the actions taken by the courts of kings, mythological narratives, and more. While some creative licence might have been involved, skaldic poetry remains one of the more reliable sources of information about the time period.

Returning briefly to Al Ewing's *Loki: Agent of Asgard* Marvel comic, there's a fine line between a lie and a story. Indeed, as Ewing's *Agent* Loki goes on a journey of self-discovery and morally ambiguous redemption, they change title (and frequently gender) from God of Mis-chief, to God of Lies, and then finally adopt the moniker God(dess) of Stories. The concluding issues #13–17 of *Loki: Agent of Asgard* see this God(dess) of Stories simultaneously contend with a metaphysical identity crisis and a more literal, action-packed Ragnarok-level crisis.

Agent Loki reminds the reader (via their best friend, lie-detecting ghost Verity) that stories are tall tales, told and retold, changing over time and periodically reborn as something different in a new place and time. There is great power in the stories we tell about who we are and where we come from; ultimately setting the scene for where we may be going in life. But we don't have to become trapped in our current narrative, just as we don't have to be trapped in the identities and/or life traject-ories that appear written for us.

This Loki can rewrite their destiny, reframe their role in the Marvel comics universe, and renew their appeal with a broader audience. *Loki: Agent of Asgard* #13 bookends with the scene from 3,000 years ago of a skald regaling a Viking Hall full of people with tales of gods and magic, as they take shelter from a fierce thunderstorm. The skald is an old man whose outfit evokes the trademark 'green and horns' associated with Marvel's Lokis, harnessing a power of his very own; the power of stories, tall tales, lies to entertain and explain away the mysteries of the young and often frightening world.

Literary fiction, whether marketed towards adults or chil-dren and young people, frequently turns towards myth-ological tricksters for inspiration. Indeed, author Neil

Gaiman has written at least three Loki variations – in his own retelling of *Norse Mythology*, disguised as a fox in *Odd and the Frost Giants*, and in the guise of Low Key Lye-smith in *American Gods*. Gaiman's fox Loki immediately carries with it the assumption of cunning, described as 'an animal with a plan' with flame-coloured hair.[2] Red hair is an often overlooked part of Loki's appearance due to the jet-black locks of the omnipresent Marvel variations, but it's actually closer to how the Norse god is depicted. It's well-established that Gaiman has done his Norse home-work. In *American Gods*, Low Key Lyesmith/Mr World has 'orange-blonde hair' and scarring around his mouth refer-encing when the *Eddas* Loki has their lips sewn shut by the dwarf Brokk. Further subtle references to the mythol-ogy can also be found in Low Key's use of matches, light-ers, and candles, leaning again towards interpretations of the *Eddas* Loki as Logi – a word translating as 'flame' and the name of a Norse giant that personified fire.[3]

A much-celebrated novel, and subsequent TV adap-tation, the key themes of *American Gods* are questions of faith and the power of ritual. Old Gods who were brought over to the United States by immigrants, are losing their powers (and in some cases, their lives) as their followers deplete in numbers, and find themselves being manoeuvred towards a battle for supremacy against New Gods of technology, media, the stock market, and more. It's finally revealed that this cold war is a conspiracy orchestrated by Odin, who wants to restore his power via the deaths of others in battle, and Loki who wants to feed off the chaos that will ensue. When Low Key explains, 'It's about being you, but the you that people believe in. [...] You take all the belief, all the prayers and they become a kind of certainty',[4] he's linking omnipotence with cultural memory.

Over the course of the 20th century, sociology, cultural anthropology, history, and other interrelated fields often returned to questions of how identity, consciousness, culture, and memory could be a shared experience – a sort of ongoing group project. Jan and Aleida Assmann, an Egyptologist and a Professor of English and Literary Studies, respectively, have been refining their understanding of the idea of cultural memory since the 1990s.[5] Cultural memory preserves a shared mythological history, stretching back to an imagined beginning of time and social reality itself. A combination of institutional and individual actions are at play; participation in group ritual, knowledge of specific stories and texts, leadership and cultural gate-keeping from specialised individuals such as priests and scholars, and the function of museums, monuments and specific objects as vessels for collective memory.[6]

Think of it this way – the kings and chieftains, and skalds and seers of the Viking Age were the keepers of all that was and could be known about the world and were important figures in ceremonial occasions. Temples and alters, and statues and runestones were sites for cultural practice, collective experiences, and social bonding. The abstract, moral and philosophical messages tied to tangible symbols would help establish a formalised framework; by which Norse people could share in a sense of group identity, collective purpose, and shared history beyond that which could be offered by two or three generations of living memory.

Thus, the divine reasoning behind the conspiracy between Low Key Lyesmith and Mr Wednesday (Odin) is correct in *American Gods*. Losing their status and legitimacy in contemporary Western cultural memory is a threat to their very existence. For them, there is literal power in myth, in stories.

Indeed, the power of stories is something shared more broadly in our own reality, from news media framing world events from certain perspectives,[7] to the lessons learned and questions asked in fiction across countless platforms. It's partly the sheer number of media platforms and the different formats that they exist in now, that has impacted on the endurance of cultural memory from older ages,[8] as well as the change in audience expectations… and demands.

It's hard to imagine the Norse skalds holding the attention of a captive audience in quite the same way these days – the oral storytelling tradition has lost some of the magical hold it once held, for instance. The bigger problem, however, is that the Norse pantheon as the *Eddas* present them are rather lacking in depth of character-isation and empathetic psychology. Contemporary story-tellers have to find ways to get inside the minds of Odin, Thor and the rest, in order to make us really care about them.[9] A trickster can be exploited for their actions as ways to further the plot, but to be engaging fiction we need writers to explore motivations, too. Frankly, we have little to go on in trying to identify or empathise with Low Key Lyesmith; he remains as much a figure built around 'doing things' as the *Eddas* Loki was.

'Lokasenna', aka 'Loki's Flyting' or 'Loki's Quarrel', is a rare example of focusing on the *Eddas* Loki's emotional and mental state. The poem describes a feast of the gods that Loki has not been invited to, taking place some-where between the death of Baldr and the binding of Loki in the cave. The *Eddas* Loki is becoming the antag-onist who will lead the charge at Ragnarök and gate-crashes the feast to verbally abuse and threaten various members of the pantheon. For readers who have follow-ed Joanne Harris's variation in her novel *The Gospel of Loki*, this outburst has been building up for some time and feels justified. The *Gospel* Loki has become increas-ingly resentful of Odin, Thor, et al. and feels he and his monstrous offspring have been treated very poorly despite everything his machinations have done for the preservation and prosperity of Asgard.

Flyting is essentially an ancient version of a rap battle, found in Norse, Celtic and Old English literature as well as having been a form of public entertainment. An insulting and confrontational verbal back and forth between individuals and/or parties, it could be ceremonial, jovial, and cathartic. Even today, in Shetland dialect the word 'flyte/flite' is still used to mean 'to scold'.[10]

Harris's *Gospel* Loki has had a few drinks before he crashes the party to flyte upon the gods, and it would be reasonable to assume that the original *Eddas* Loki had too. Accusations of cowardice, infidelity, incest, perversion, stupidity, and more are flung around, and by the end any gods that still felt any goodwill towards Loki have also turned against the trickster.

In Klas Östergren's novel *Orkanpartyt*, or *The Hurricane Party*, we find what appears to be Sweden in the grip of a harsh economic and ecological dystopia. A man's search for his son in this grim environment leads us to discover that the mob family who control everything are in fact the Norse gods, and there follows an extended version of 'Lokasenna' as a mob dinner where Loki is a manipulative, psychopathic gangster.[11] It's… not for everyone, and I'm not sure it's one for me, but it's such an odd direction to take things in that I couldn't not mention it. This mob flyting is recounted for many, many pages retelling much of the mythology one might already be familiar with, just using colourful language evoking *The Sopranos* TV series.

Loki's Flyting is one of the more adult-themed episodes in Norse mythology, and yet Loki variations appear to lend themselves particularly well to books for children and young adults. The persistent themes of rebellion, mischief-making, shapeshifting outsiders, fantastic adventure, and clever wordplay are appealing to readers of all ages. One would imagine that Loki often proves invaluable in encouraging reading for pleasure in young people.

The 1975 children's fantasy novel *Eight Days of Luke* by Diana Wynne Jones is told from the perspective of orphan David. During the summer holidays from school, David meets an exciting and mysterious red-haired boy called Luke who claims to have been released from a magical prison involving chains and bowls of venom, and who David can summon by merely lighting a flame. The novel becomes a slow-burn coming-of-age mystery in which David has to compete with his extended family of especially useless and objectionable people, alongside protecting his new pyromaniac friend from strangers who sound uncannily familiar. All these new people in

David's life are not explicitly identified as certain Norse gods until quite late in the novel, though we're given clues to their identities as they search for something important.

Spending time with Luke offers David an escape from his unhappy personal circumstances, and enough of a glimpse of a more rebellious and risky life that he proves himself to be more resourceful and resilient than he thought he was. It also reminds young readers to be careful what you wish for, a recurring cautionary takeaway in many Loki variations.

The Marvel machine is working hard to reach young readers too, with the likes of the aforementioned queer young adult novel *Loki: Where Mischief Lies*, and the short graphic novel *Thor & Loki: Double Trouble* which is intentionally suitable for readers of all ages.

One might wonder, however, what of the children who encounter Norse Mythology in something more closely approximating the *Eddas*? Let's be honest, there's a reason why retellings and variations are specifically produced for younger readers – kids in the school library, like I was. How might a child process all of the binding by entrails and inter-species procreation? The semi-autobiographical 2011 novel *Ragnarok: The End of The Gods*, by A.S. Byatt, is part environmental disaster allegory (as the Netflix teen series *Ragnarok* is, too) and part experience of a child discovering Norse Mythology against the backdrop of the Second World War. Referred to only as the Thin Child, a young girl grapples with the almost unimaginable tales of the gods and their outlandish conflicts; while trying to simultaneously mythologise and rationalise the very real war that saw her evacuated to the countryside. Anxiety and denial are the overarching feelings that the Thin Child picks up on as she reads about Odin et al., go on adventures and Wild Hunts, enjoy excessive revelry, and battle monstrous beings, while all the while the pantheon are fully aware that they live on borrowed time. As the end of all things approaches with Ragnarök, the Thin Child can identify with the fear and uncertainty of assumed impending doom.

Described in one analysis as being a scientist,[12] Byatt's Loki is driven by his curiosity and an amorality that sees him live a life without consequence. Or at least, the illusion of a life without consequence, because the Thin Child reads this variation as an inventor and explorer whose actions (and lack thereof) start a series of chain reactions culminating in the prophesised end of everything. Though clever, Byatt's Loki cannot see the impact of his child, the Midgard Serpent, continuing to grow and consume much of the life and habitat of the World Ocean. This Loki prefers to shapeshift and swim around with her; either oblivious or uninterested in the roles his various monstrous offspring are destined to play and ultimately die because of.

Byatt's novel deftly interweaves the Norse tall tales with the very real war, throughout the book. Neither the gods nor the human race strictly *have* to doom themselves to destruction, but it's hard to see how either can recover when their complacency and hubris have led them to the brink. It's an interesting and philosophically compelling premise, albeit an unsettling story due to its timeless message.

Another particularly interesting (but quite different) story of late, is where writer and illustrator Louie Stowell has struck gold with her books *Loki: A Bad God's Guide to Being Good* and *...A Bad God's Guide to Taking the Blame*, with a further *...Guide to Ruling the World* making three, with more to come. By trapping the immortal deity in the body of an eleven-year-old boy and making him go to school as a punishment from Odin, we might have found ourselves the Loki that the youth of this generation could internalise as their own. I do hope so. This *Bad God* Loki shares their thoughts and feelings via the magical diary format of Stowell's books; complete with lie detector, regular Loki Virtue Score (LVS) updates (it's pretty much always plummeting into negative figures), and wonderfully childish doodles. It's clear throughout that Stowell has been passionately researching the original mythology and frequently refers to parts of the *Eddas* Loki's exploits that may be considered too subversive for other variations.

Bad God Loki delights in reminding his peers about when he was a horse, for example, and gave birth to Sleipnir – 'Believe me, growing a being inside you is deeply uncomfortable. Especially when your baby has eight legs to kick you with.'[13] Many of the stranger events of Norse mythology are either referred to off-hand or feature as key plot-points, finding just the right kind of offbeat details that can engage and entertain young people. This is a Loki variation who hasn't yet taken a truly evil turn (*Bad God* Loki hasn't killed Baldr at this point, and there are still a few adventures to be had before Ragnarök)[14] which allows for further exploration of what constitutes good and bad. There are lessons in morality and empathy alongside the funny drawings and frequent occurrence of the word 'turd'.

And importantly, there is an honesty in Stowell's books, a kind of honesty that is often gifted to children but that tends to unnerve adults who are invested in the status quo. Capitalism, private school, colonialism, the police, sexism, and other elements of the modern world are given short shrift as part of the social justice subtext of these books. Quite fitting that a Loki variation can help rebellious youngsters question and mock the institutions that exert power over them.

*

The stories that can be told with Loki variations are many and diverse; fittingly able to shapeshift as required. Arriving at this near-end point, it's hopefully become clear that the importance of the variations is as much in the stories they tell, and what we can take from them, as it is in who their audience is. There are almost instinctive qualities in the tall tales that Loki can tell as the God of Stories. Escapism and wish-fulfilment. Catharsis and reflection. Truth and lies. Perhaps most significantly, Loki can tell stories about identity and belonging.

We've a better grasp of the manifold stories Loki is a vessel to tell, but are we actually any closer to knowing who the 'real' Loki is?

(Dis)Honourable Mentions

In the process of researching and pulling together Loki variations, there were some that I truthfully just didn't know what to do with, or how they could possibly be consolidated into the four 'God of…' themes that I've divined. But one of them might be your variation, or you might just get a kick out of knowing that they exist (and frustrate me), so to that end, I present to you:

- Matt Damon's fallen angel Loki, in the movies *Dogma* and *Jay and Silent Bob Reboot*. The former Angel of Death, now banished to Wisconsin by God (who looks exactly like Canadian singer-songwriter Alanis Morrisette), Damon's Loki plots to return to Heaven with his friend Bartleby (played by Ben Affleck). There's no connection to Norse mythology at all. He just has the same name. That's it, really.

- Matt Damon's Actor Loki, in the movies *Thor: Ragnarok* and *Thor: Love and Thunder*, where he portrays Loki in a play repainting the 'fallen' MCU Loki as the hero in the story to entertain the masses... in front of Loki, who's in fact disguised as Odin. He returns as a true thespian caricature in the latter, dramatising the previous film in theatrical form. It's a weird cameo that sums up the tone of these MCU entries.
- Matt Da– no, wait, I'm kidding.
- The 2005 Danish children's TV advent calendar series *Jul I Valhal*, or, *Christmas in Valhalla*. 24 episodes (one aired each day in the run-up to Christmas) telling the story of a couple of kids who try to help catch Loki and prevent Ragnarök before Christmas. Based on episode summaries and the snippets of video available online, this sounds like it was... Well, quite something. See if you can find 'Loke's Rapsody/Loki's Rhapsody' with subtitles, on YouTube...
- Finally, we need to address the 2005 follow-up to the questionable '90s Jim Carrey hit movie *The Mask*. A sequel almost certainly regretted by everyone involved, *Son of The Mask* is one of the worst films in the history of human culture.[1] Imagine being a film studio with 90 minutes to fill and an $84 million budget, and deciding to spend

it on a terrifying CGI baby, a Wile E. Coyote rip-off CGI dog, GREEN CGI SPERM WITH FACES INCLUDING TEETH, an elaborate music medley, a garishly modified 'hero' car, Bob Hoskins as Odin (disguised under considerable make-up and costuming), and Scottish actor Alan Cumming as Loki. I'm not making this up. I wish I was. I'm so sorry if you didn't already know this existed. The *Son of The Mask* Loki, if you even still care at this point, is a God of Mischief with daddy issues and an inflated ego who needs to recover the mask that harnesses his chaotic powers. The son of Odin in this variation is dressed like a rejected nu-metal band lead singer, portrayed as being both campy sinister and cartoonishly violent, kidnaps the aforementioned baby to play twister with him, and for some reason talks with an affected American accent. Again, this is a genuine thing that exists in our reality.

This is just a snapshot of some of the Loki variations that deviate more significantly from the *Eddas* source material. Perhaps more accurately described as Loki *deviations*, they serve as somewhat unfortunate obstacles to uncovering a better understanding of who Loki is.

I need to go and lie down in a dark room for a wee minute and suggest that you do the same.

Conclusion

'How should Loki be referred to?' Snorri's *Prose Edda* asks.

'By calling him the son of Farbauti and Laufey or Nal, the brother of Byleist and Helblindi,' it continues. 'The father of the spewer of the river Van, who is the wolf Fenrir, the father of Jormungand, who is the Midgard Serpent, the father of Hel and Nari, the kinsman and father's brother of Ali, the comrade and bench mate of Odin and the Æsir, the guest of Geirrod, the adornment of Geirrod's wooden chest, one who steals from giants, the thief of the goat, of Idunn's apples, and of the rings of the Brisings, the kinsman of Sleipnir, the husband of Sigyn, the foe of the gods, the wrecker of Sif's hair, the author of woes, the sly god, the one who slanders and betrays the gods, the one who engineered Baldr's death, the bound one and the vexing litigant against Hemdall and Skaldi.'[1]

That is all good and well for this variation, but it doesn't really answer the question: Who *is* Loki?

In these earlier forms, the moralistic censoring of the more pagan, ambiguous, subversive, and non-conforming elements of Norse mythology were either sanitised or used to turn Loki into a Lucifer-esque stand-in without justification in the narrative. They're neither a hero, nor a villain.

Loki is queer — or at least, that's our word for it. They wouldn't actually need to have a term to describe themselves in relation to gender, sexuality, and romantic feelings because it would be redundant for a shape-shifting, omnipotent immortal who had birthed several offspring of different natures.

Loki is a God of Knots. From the moment they took a blood oath with Odin they were entwined not only with the Norse pantheon, but with the very fabric of their world and its destiny. Loki's actions are central to how the *Eddas* play out from the creation of the Nine Worlds to their end at Ragnarök. Loki's tricks, half-truths, machinations, and children are part of a chain of events including: accompanying Odin and Thor, as a friend, on their adventures; ensuring that Asgard's defensive walls were built; orchestrating both the kidnap and rescue of the goddess Idunn; commissioning the gifts made by the dwarves; engineering the death of Baldr; and finally leading the charge of monsters, giants, demons and the undead against Asgard. But Loki's actions are not black-and-white. They have a complicated, multi-layered relationship with the rest of the Norse gods and have some complex feelings about their place and identity among them. Loki gets tangled up in situations that they cannot cleanly get out of. And there are consequences, as in our own reality; further strands that lead in different directions.

Loki is clever. It's a certain kind of smart, being clever. It's being intelligent and talented, but also particularly quick to learn and react, with original and shrewd solutions. Clever is cunning and it is emotional. Loki is the most engaging figure in Norse mythology because they are the most developed character in terms of personality and recognisable emotions. Granted, there's limited competition (oh look, Thor is drunk and hasn't considered an appropriate response, again); but in Loki we have someone to imprint upon, to align with, and to escape to. It's not surprising, then, that there are so many Loki variations out there.

Who is Loki? Loki is many things. Loki is not a single construct and has no single message – a vessel for much and a tall tale to teach many lessons. An immortal, metaphysical shapeshifter, they're an elusive, adaptable, and therefore enduring figure. Loki is whoever we need them to be.

Who is *your* Loki?

I bet it's Alan Cumming playing Loki in the cinematic equivalent of the Hindenburg that is *Son of The Mask*, isn't it? No? Huh.

For many it will be a Marvel variation, perhaps most likely Tom Hiddleston's MCU Loki, the most visible of recent years. There is an entire generation of people in the Western world who have grown up with him as their Loki, as the face and voice (and helmet) of the trickster as God of Mischief. From an outsider's perspective, it seems as though Hiddleston has some recognition of the scale of impact he has on popular culture, and it's to his credit that he knows that ultimately Loki is bigger than him. He is but one, albeit prominent, variation. We've only scratched the surface of all the variations across a lifetime of Marvel comics, movies, TV shows, cartoons, games, toys, and books; let alone those more widely known – but that's for another day. What does stand out to me, having gone through my notes, is how the editorial decision to have Marvel's Loki and Thor be brothers has influenced other interpretations of Loki across pop culture. The cynic (and apparently the over-protective Loki fan) in me would politely suggest that some folk need to do their homework, properly. The de-aged and more openly queer Loki(s) of Marvel comics in recent years has struck an important note of recognition and inclusion, and that shouldn't be taken lightly in a world where comics are still too quickly dismissed as mindless fluff.

For some, the medium in which their Loki resides may be just as important as the message they bring. The form and genre in which a Loki variation exists, and the audience who are most likely to consume this, are important contextual factors. In this respect, your variation may be presented via a cultural format/genre that carries discrediting or stigmatising associations. We've touched on some, but every format will have their own Loki to discover and hopefully enjoy regardless of the prejudices of others.

The variations in games (and their expansions) like *God of War* and *Assassin's Creed: Valhalla* are often intended as plot drivers to lead action and complete objectives, rather than allowing for the depth a several-decade evolution can offer. To some extent they have the burden of franchise to align with, yet they can also serve as gateways to other texts. On television, the long-form approach of shows like *Supernatural* and *The Almighty Johnsons* allows for some blurring of genre lines, but also comes with the expectations of studios and pressure from ratings. In books, fiction faces similar challenges to an extent but in terms of plot are freer to explore without the burden of budget constraints on the creativity within. In literary form, Loki variants can rule over grim, sprawling dystopias, or battle frost giants in between school lessons. They can walk us over whatever Bifrost rainbow bridge we can conjure in our minds and exert a subconscious influence on other Middle Earths and Iron Thrones.

For the most part, all these different variations can serve as cautionary tales, satisfy wish fulfillment, inspire confidence, lead us to question authority, and aid in self-discovery. It's an interesting and not insignificant strength of Loki that their variations so often appeal to children and young adults, offering a kindred spirit of sorts. Some other examples are purely entertaining and an opportunity to switch off from the voices in one's head. Maybe it all depends on whether you were one of those 'mythology kids' in school.

Maybe you already know your Loki variation well and have had them by your side for years. Maybe you're still discovering more of them in your quest for that one singular, chosen Loki. Maybe their purpose is clear to you. Maybe they still have one last trick to show you. Whichever Loki is yours; I hope they bring you comfort, confidence, questions, and answers.

So, back to that age old question: who is *my* Loki, and what is their glorious purpose?

We come around almost full circle but not quite, the terrain and the narrative now is something familiar yet different from what we started with. Some of the figures are the same but there are also new players on the board. The Ragnarök cycle of birth, death and rebirth can be a personal as well as a metaphysical one; it is through self-reflection, discovery, and sharing stories that we learn more about who we are and what matters to us.

I'll always return, first and foremost, to the *Eddas* Loki – that's who I first encountered in the school library and everything that has come after is essentially fanfiction in one sense or another. Joanne Harris's *Gospel* Loki very convincingly fills in some gaps in the relatively limited prose and poetry that we have to go on. The *Gospel* Loki makes sense to me in explaining some (though, perhaps not all) of what motivates Loki and what internal struggles they face.

There's also a lot of Marvel in my Loki – not the MCU Loki specifically, but rather the variations in Marvel comics. They provide accompanying details for me in terms of what the *Eddas* Loki might be doing now, if they found a way to survive Ragnarök and took full advantage of all the modern world has to offer. I can't escape seeing the trademark 'green and horns' in my mind, but there's a kind of truth in the tall tales of Marvel comic's queer, chaotic, antihero searching for a better sense of self and purpose, and enjoying the spoils every now and then.

As a result of the field I work in, I can't help but look beyond the surface and so am fascinated by the kinds of social, cultural, and political connections that can be made between Loki's reality and our own. There wasn't space here to explore the substantial (if at times problematic) academic works by Jan de Vries[2] and Anna Birgitta Rooth,[3] that seek to critically examine the supposedly 'true' cultural and mythological roots of the trickster in a not dissimilar manner to myself here (though theirs are far, far drier). Or the satire of the 2016 Marvel comic *Vote Loki*, which comments on the impact of the lies we accept as an electorate, from those with all of the power and none of the responsibility. As we've said, the variations never truly end.

With the space that we did have here, though, my hope is that I've given you some food for thought in relation to what is effectively my imaginary friend. My Loki reminds us not to simply defer to perceived authority or seniority without questioning and holding power to account; while also serving as a warning for what happens if you go too far. My Loki can start conversations about belonging and discrimination, about who and what we choose to follow, and about morality and subjugation.

My Loki gave birth to a horse, and just owns it.

References

Introduction

1. Snorri Sturluson, *The Prose Edda*. Penguin Classics, 2005 (1220).
2. Callum Brown, *Up-helly-aa: Custom, Culture and Community in Shetland*. Manchester University Press, 1998.
3. Ibid.
4. Ibid.
5. Chris Barker & Emma A. Jane, *Cultural Studies: Theory and practice 5th ed*. SAGE, 2016.
6. Theodor Adorno & Max Horkheimer, *Dialectic of Enlightenment*. Herder and Herder,1972 (1947).
7. Naomi Barnes & Alison Bedford, *Unlocking Social Theory with Popular Culture: Remixing Theoretical Influencers*. Springer, 2021.
8. Stuart Hall, *Encoding and Decoding in the Television Discourse*. Centre for Contemporary Cultural Studies, Birmingham, 1973.
9. Roland Barthes, *Mythologies*. Paladin, 1972 (1957).
10. Curtis, N. (2021). Superheroes and the mythic imagination: order, agency and politics. Journal of Graphic Novels and Comics, 12(5), 360-374. doi.org/10.1080/21504857.2019.1690015
11. "Babies' First Names" *National Records of Scotland*. nrscotland.gov.uk/statistics-and-data/statistics/statistics-by-theme/vital-events/names/babies-first-names. Accessed 17 August 2022.
12. "Top baby names of 2021" Sophie Bell, *babycentre.co.uk*, November 2021. babycentre.co.uk/top-baby-names. Accessed 17 August 2022.

Chapter 1: God of Knots

1. Snorri Sturluson, *The Prose Edda*. Penguin Classics, 2005 (1220).
2. Ibid.
3. Kevin Crossley-Holland, *The Norse Myths*. Pantheon Books, 1980.
4. Ibid.
5. Kevin Crossley-Holland, *Norse Myths: Tales of Odin, Thor and Loki*. Walker Studio, 2017.
6. "An introduction to The Gospel of Loki from Joanne Harris" Joanne Harris, *joanne-harris.co.uk*. joanne-harris.co.uk/books/the-gospel-of-loki/read-an-introduction-to-the-gospel-of-loki-from-joanne-harris/. Accessed 17 August 2022.
7. von Schnurbein, S. (2000). The Function of Loki in Snorri Sturluson's "Edda." History of Religions, 40(2), 109–124. doi.org/10.1086/463618
8. Jan de Vries, *The Problem of Loki*. Suomalainen Tiedeakatemia, 1933.
9. Heide, E. (2011). Loki, the "Vätte", and the Ash Lad: A Study Combining Old Scandinavian and Late Material. Viking and Medieval Scandinavia, 7, 63–106. doi.org/10.1484/J.VMS.1.102616
10. Ibid.
11. Louie Stowell, *Loki: A Bad God's Guide to Being Good*. Walker Books, 2022.
12. Bassil-Morozow, H. (2017). Loki then and now: the trickster against civilization, International Journal of Jungian Studies, 9(2), 84-96. doi.org/10.1080/19409052.2017.1309780
13. Ibid.

Chapter 2: God of Mischief

1. Stan Lee & Jack Kirby, *Journey Into Mystery #111*. Marvel, 1962.

2. "LOKI: HOW MARVEL COMICS TURNED ITS MOST SELFISH VILLAIN INTO A HERO" Grame McMillan, *Inverse*, 28 May 2021. inverse.com/entertainment/loki-hero-or-villain-comic-book-history. Accessed 17 August 2022.

3. Henry Jenkins, *Convergence Culture: Where old and new media collide*. NYU Press, 2006.

4. "Transmedia 202: Further Reflections" Henry Jenkins, *henryjenkins.org*, 31 July 2011. henryjenkins.org/2011/08/defining_transmedia_further_re.html. Accessed 17 August 2022.

5. "Tom Hiddleston Says He's a 'Temporary Torchbearer' Playing Loki" K.J. Yossman, *Variety*, 2 March 2022. variety.com/2022/tv/news/loki-tom-hiddleston-sophia-dimartino-1235194488/. Accessed 17 August 2022.

6. Douglas Wolk, *All of the Marvels: An Amazing Voyage into Marvel's Universe and 27,000 Superhero Comics*. Profile Books, 2021.

7. "LOKI: HOW MARVEL COMICS TURNED ITS MOST SELFISH VILLAIN INTO A HERO" Grame McMillan, Inverse, 28 May 2021. inverse.com/entertainment/loki-hero-or-villain-comic-book-history. Accessed 17 August 2022.

8. Jason Aaron, Al Ewing, & Simone Bianchi. *Original Sin #5.5*. Marvel, 2014.

9. "Loki's Sexuality and Gender Fluidity in Comics" Marlene Bonnelly, *The Mary Sue*, 21 June 2018. themarysue.com/loki-sexuality-gender-fluidity/. Accessed 17 August 2022.

10. Curtis, N., & Cardo, V. (2018). Superheroes and third-wave feminism. Feminist Media Studies, 18(3), 381-396. doi.org/10.1080/14680777.2017.1351387

11. Stein, D (2018) Bodies in transition. Queering the Comic Book Superhero. Navigationen. 1(S), 15–38. DOI: doi.org/10.25969/mediarep/1832

12. Annamarie Jagose, *Queer Theory: An Introduction*. NYU Press, 1996.

13. Khayatt, D. (2002). Toward a Queer Identity. Sexualities, 5(4), 487-501. doi.org/10.1177/1363460702005004006

14. Althaus-Reid, M., & Isherwood, L. (2007). Thinking Theol-

ogy and Queer Theory. Feminist Theology, 15(3), 302-314. https://doi.org/10.1177/0966735006076168

15.   Annamarie Jagose, *Queer Theory: An Introduction*. NYU Press, 1996.

16.   "On Loki, Anti-Heroes, and Who Gets to Be a Lovable Villain" Stich, *Teen Vogue*, 21 July 2021. teenvogue.com/story/on-loki-anti-heroes-and-who-gets-to-be-a-lovable-villain-fanservice. Accessed 17 August 2022.

17.   Bassil-Morozow, H. (2017). Loki then and now: the trickster against civilization, International Journal of Jungian Studies, 9(2), 84-96. https://doi.org/10.1080/19409052.2017.1309780

18.   Snorri Sturluson, *The Prose Edda*. Penguin Classics, 2005.

19.   "From Myth to MCU, Loki Was Always Queer" Clint Worthington, *The Companion*, 23 June 2021. thecompanion.app/2021/06/23/from-myth-to-mcu-loki-was-always-queer/. Accessed 17 August 2022.

20.   "Marvel's Got a New YA Novel About Loki Coming Out, and It's Going to Be Queer as Hell" Marykate Jasper, *The Mary Sue*, 12 December 2017. themarysue.com/marvel-ya-novel-loki-genderfluid-pan/. Accessed 17 August 2022.

Chapter 3: God of Outcasts

1.   Joanne Harris, *The Gospel of Loki*. Gollancz, 2014.

2.   Howard S. Becker, *Outsiders: Studies in the Sociology of Deviance*. Free Press, 1963.

3.   Erving Goffman, *Stigma: Notes on the Management of Spoiled Identity*. Penguin Books, 1968.

4.   Lopes, P. (2006). Culture and Stigma: Popular Culture and the Case of Comic Books. Sociological Forum, 21(3), 387–414. https://doi.org/10.1007/s11206-006-9022-6

5.   "Manga belongs in the British Museum as much as the Elgin marbles" David Barnett, *The Guardian*, 23 May 2019. theguardian.com/commentisfree/2019/may/23/manga-british-museum-elgin-marbles. Accessed 17 August 2022.

6. Henry Jenkins, *Textual Poachers: Television Fans & Participatory Culture*. Routledge, 1992.

7. Jonathan Gray, Cornel Sandvoss, & C. Lee Harrington, *Fandom: Identities and Communities in a Mediated World 2nd ed*. NYU Press, 2017.

8. Elliott, M.A. (2021). Fandom as religion: A social-scientific assessment. The Journal of Fandom Studies, 9(2), 107-122. doi.org/10.1386/jfs_00036_1

9. Matt Hills, *Fan Cultures*. Routledge, 2002.

10. Daniel Kibblesmith, Ozgur Yildirim, & Andy MacDonald, *Loki: The God Who Fell to Earth #5*. Marvel, 2019.

11. Ibid.

12. "I gave a panel of @kibblesmith incredible comic to Tom on our first day of shooting. Thanks for letting us use your words Daniel and writing Loki so beautifully ❤" @iamkateherron. *Twitter*, 11 July 2021, 12:03 AM, twitter.com/iamkateherron/status/1413997448310177793. Accessed 17 August 2022.

13. "How Do We Define Fandom? Moving Beyond the Transformative vs. Curatorial Binary" Stitch, *Teen Vogue*, 16 March 2021. teenvogue.com/story/how-do-we-define-fandom-stitch-fan-service. Accessed 17 August 2022.

14. Jonathan Gray, Cornel Sandvoss, & C. Lee Harrington, *Fandom: Identities and Communities in a Mediated World 2nd ed*. NYU Press, 2017.

Chapter 4: God of Stories

1. "Collection: Sociology & Literature" *The Sociological Review*, March 2016 to March 2019. thesociologicalreview.org/collections/sociology-and-literature/. Accessed 17 August 2022.

2. Neil Gaiman & Brett Helquist, *Odd and the Frost Giants*. Bloomsbury, 2008.

3. Jan de Vries, *The Problem of Loki*. Suomalainen Tiedeakatemia, 1933.

4. Ibid.
5. Astrid Erll, *Memory in Culture*. Palgrave Macmillan, 2011.
6. Astrid Erll & Ansgar Nünning, *Cultural Memory Studies: An International and Interdisciplinary Handbook*. De Gruyter, 2010.
7. Pan, Z., & Kosicki, G.M. (1993). Framing analysis: An approach to news discourse. Political Communication, 10(1), 55-75. DOI: 10.1080/10584609.1993.9962963
8. Astrid Erll, *Memory in Culture*. Palgrave Macmillan, 2011.
9. Hume, K. (2019) Loki and Odin: Old Gods Repurposed by Neil Gaiman, A. S. Byatt, and Klas Östergren. Studies in the Novel, 51(2), 297-310. doi:10.1353/sdn.2019.0033.
10. Alastair Christie-Johnston & Adaline Christie-Johnston, *Shetland Words: A dictionary of the Shetland dialect, revised edition*. The Shetland Times Ltd, 2014.
11. Klas Östergren, *The Hurricane Party*. Canongate, 2007.
12. Hume, K. (2019) Loki and Odin: Old Gods Repurposed by Neil Gaiman, A. S. Byatt, and Klas Östergren. Studies in the Novel, 51(2), 297-310. doi:10.1353/sdn.2019.0033.
13. Louie Stowell, *Loki: A Bad God's Guide to Taking the Blame*. Walker Books, 2022.
14. "Interview: Louie Stowell on Loki: A Bad God's Guide to being Good - Fart jokes and fake parents" *Imagining History*, 5 September 2022. imagininghistory.co.uk/post/interview-author-louie-stowell-on-loki-a-bad-god-s-guide-to-being-good. Accessed 17 September 2022.

(Dis)Honourable Mentions

1. "SON OF THE MASK" *Rotten Tomatoes*, exact date unknown. rottentomatoes.com/m/son_of_the_mask. Accessed 17 August 2022.

Conclusion

1. Snorri Sturluson, *The Prose Edda*. Penguin Classics, 2005 (1220).
2. Jan de Vries, *The Problem of Loki*. Suomalainen Tiedeakatemia, 1933.
3. Anna Birgitta Rooth, *Loki in Scandinavian Mythology*. C. W. K. Gleerup, 1961.

Acknowledgements

Thank you, Heather and Laura, for taking a chance on whatever this is and for being so patient.

Thank you, Luke, for the image that couldn't have been anything else.

Thank you, Thom, for the kindness and encouragement of someone who knows.

Thank you, Harriet and Martin, for a conversation you almost definitely won't remember.

Thank you, John, for this being a possibility at all.

Thank you, Linnea, for the insider knowledge.

Thank you, Roisin, Fraser, and Morag, for popping your heads round the door to bother me.

Thank You, for being here.

About the Author

Karl Johnson is a lecturer in Sociology, a life-long geek, and a Shetlander trapped in the Central Belt of Scotland. He researches and writes about widening access to higher education, social theory and pop culture, and issues affecting the Scottish Islands – such as gendered exclusion in Lerwick's Up Helly Aa festival.

Twitter: @karlpjohnson

About the Inklings series

This book is part of 404 Ink's Inkling series which presents big ideas in pocket-sized books.

They are all available at 404ink.com/shop.

If you enjoyed this book, you may also enjoy these titles in the series:

Now Go – Karl Thomas Smith

Now Go enters the emotional waters to interrogate not only how Studio Ghibli navigates grief, but how that informs our own understanding of its manifold faces.

Love That Journey For Me – Emily Garside

Considering the fusion of existing sitcom traditions, references and tropes, this Inkling analyses the nuance of *Schitt's Creek* and its surrounding cultural and societal impact as a queer revolution.